Quintessential Bellydance

Evgenia Karmi

WOTS 2016

Terpsichore
Muse of Dance
Daughter of Olympian Zeus and Titan Mnemosyne
Inspiration, dedication, manifestation
I live vicariously, yet I am fully realized
Terpsichore
Greek Goddess of delightful dance and choral song
Meetera to the seductive Sirens with their hypnotic voices
Terpsichore
Everlasting kindred spirit

Evyenia Karmi

Quintessential Bellydance

BEGINNER CLASS COMPANION

Evyenia Karmi

iUniverse LLC
Bloomington

iUniverse books may be ordered through booksellers or by contacting:

iUniverse LLC
1663 Liberty Drive
Bloomington, IN 47403
www.iuniverse.com
1-800-Authors (1-800-288-4677)

Photos by megapixproductions.com

ISBN: 978-1-4759-4787-8 (sc)
ISBN: 978-1-4759-4788-5 (hc)
ISBN: 978-1-4759-4789-2 (ebk)

Printed in the United States of America

iUniverse rev. date: 08/09/2013

This book is for my beloved parents, Basile and Olymbia,
and my supportive brother, Demetrios.

Thank you for allowing me freedom of expression
to be the artist I am today.

I age learning something new every day.

—Solon, Greek statesman circa 600 BC

Foreword

Tasso Lakas
TV Variety Producer-Writer

The first time I experienced a live bellydance performance was in a Greek nightclub in Greenwich Village in New York City. At the time, I was a teenager from a small factory city in Canada and very much involved in the arts, including dance, so this was a very eye-opening experience. A few decades later, two things stand out in my memory: the energy and excitement that consumed all the club patrons when the bellydancer energetically glided onto the club floor through a myriad of tables, and the overwhelming beauty of the dance and the dancer.

I was completely mesmerized with the finger cymbals keeping to the beat of the music, the allure of the body dressed in layers of colourful silk, the smiling and seductive face, and the controlled movements of the bellydancer's body. I could only imagine what it would be like to know who this mysterious woman was with all her feminine charms. Bellydancers are seductive and mysterious creatures who fascinate Westerners with this Eastern Mediterranean dance.

But that was then and this is now. Bellydancers gracefully express their femininity in dance and movement and strike up the feeling of a never-ending awe among a much broader audience now that consists of men, women, and children. They are no longer limited to clubs. Bellydance shows are now much more common in theatres, restaurants, and family gatherings. Even so, we are all still mesmerized by the rhythms, contortions, and excitement of these performers draped in veils. They are as mysterious and alluring as ever.

Speaking purely from a male perspective, I say that any woman who can master bellydance has a talent she can proudly demonstrate throughout her life. It will celebrate power and stature, and it will elevate her self-confidence when she interprets the narrative behind this beautiful and exotic dance.

Evyenia Karmi understands this in an understated way. This instruction book will not only keep women fit with a low-impact exercise, but it will instil self-esteem that will endure a lifetime.

tassolakas@gmail.com

Preface

A studio setting is best to learn any kind of dance. This book is intended as a class companion and as an introduction for those curious about this beautiful dance form. It is a short compilation of my instructional notes for beginner bellydance, composed of the fundamental steps that can be used in various combinations and to create choreography. This is the essential vocabulary and definition for beginner bellydance.

Each section consists of dance steps and the breakdown of the dance steps, followed by the corresponding picture; it's much like a dictionary. Some of the dance steps will be easier to learn than others, but eventually you will master all of them. Use this book as a handy reference guide following your bellydance classes.

I have arranged these moves into eight sessions; it's just like the course outline that I teach during the year. It is a good idea to read through the book first. You can also make notes on each of the session pages.

Remember, this dance form is not only beautiful and graceful but an excellent form of exercise, as well. Its fluid, gentle movements also improve coordination.

So practise, perfect, create choreography—and dance at your next social event!

Introduction

For centuries, dance has been a vital form of expression and entertainment. From the streets to family celebrations and the theatre, dance continues to unite cultures and nations. Bellydance, being one of the oldest dance forms, has finally received the recognition it deserves onstage.

Dancing has always been a part of my life. As a child I learned Greek folklore, and I also loved mimicking old Hollywood musicals on TV. While I was growing up in downtown Toronto, one of my favourite pastimes was watching the dancers from the National Ballet School across the street. When the doors opened during the hot summer months, you could be sure I was crouched in the doorway amidst the onlookers. At school dances, my friends and I would choreograph steps to popular music and even performed a couple of them onstage at the end of the year.

My parents decided to move back to Greece when my brother and I were children. We lived with my father's side of the family in the city of Drama, in the north, which was different from my mother's small town, Dorio, in the south. During the population exchange between Greece and Turkey in 1923, many of the Greeks from Pontos, Asia Minor (now Turkey), settled in northern Greece, bringing with them a culture of their own. Music, cuisine, and dialect were some of the differences we were exposed to on a daily basis, including the Turkish language. Six months later we would return to Canada, but I remember how my father loved to sing old songs from that era while he worked on the car or the house. My mum would sing along with him on many occasions, keeping him company and lending a hand.

Although my formal career in dance began many years later, it never felt as though I were learning something new but rather something familiar. Of course it took practice, because in bellydance sometimes appearances can be deceiving. The commitment to the genre came naturally, as did my contribution to this community that I am proud to belong to on both sides of the Atlantic.

I look forward to the future, with the next generation of dancers continuing to create and prosper with traditional and fusion bellydance—honouring the old world and inviting in the new.

WARM-UP

When starting any new exercise regime, it is recommended that you check with your physician first.

You should wear comfortable clothing, such as yoga pants, a T-shirt, and ballet slippers, or you can go barefoot. Wrap a scarf around your hips so you can see the movements better.

My students' ages have ranged from eight to seventy-seven years, and they have come from all walks of life. I have selected a warm-up that is easy for everyone to do. In class I do a full warm-up, but I have selected some exercises for you to do at home. Having said that, the best warm-up consists of exercises that *you* like best. These should be at least five to eight minutes long.

Torso: Twist your torso forward from side to side.
Arms and Shoulders: Roll your shoulders forward and backward.
Hands: Fan your fingers and make circles with your hands. Reverse.
Fingers: Point only the fingers up and down a few times. Gently pull back on each finger.
Lower Body: March in place by bringing your knees up to waist level and pointing your toes.
Thighs: With feet wide apart, toes outward, bend the knees and squeeze the glutes, coming up without arching your back.
Feet: Make circles with your toes. Reverse.
Calves: Alternate coming up onto the balls of your feet in a prance.
Neck: Hand behind your neck, roll your head around. Reverse.

ORIENTATION

I have divided this book into sections on Basic Arm Movements, Upper Body, Lower Body, Directional Steps, Travelling Steps, and Veil for ease of reading and comprehension. Use the Sessions part of the book for your weekly practice and to make notes. Typically, in a studio setting, I would teach a movement from the upper body and lower body, a directional step, and a travelling step. I would use these movements in a variety of combinations and eventually to create choreography.

Stand in front of a mirror and notice the four corners of the room. In bellydance, these are commonly referred to as the *diagonals*. In front, you have the left diagonal and the right diagonal. Behind, you have the back left diagonal and the back right diagonal. We are often facing one of the front diagonals (showing a three-quarter profile) when dancing, because it presents a nice long line for this dance.

Posture is so important. The easiest way to monitor your posture for bellydance is to shift your pelvis to neutral. With your feet slightly apart, look at your profile in the mirror. Your pelvis should be positioned directly underneath you. This means your pelvis *should not* be tilting forward so that you are leaning backward. Likewise, your pelvis *should not* be tilting backward so that you are leaning forward. With your pelvis in a neutral position, everything else will align naturally.

Your knees should be relaxed and *not* locked behind you. Breathe normally as you move.

- Feet face forward.
- Relax the shoulders so that they are not hunched.
- The hands also play an important role. Although they appear graceful and elegant, there is a strength and energy coming from the hands. They should be slightly fanned, with the thumb close to the index finger.
- Remember to point your toes when dancing.

Smile!

Quick Review

Posture

Posture elements consist of the following, and will be referred to throughout the book.

- Keep the feet slightly apart with the toes forward.
- Relax the knees so that they are not locked behind you.
- Shift the pelvis to neutral so that it is underneath you and not tilting forward or backward.
- Relax the shoulders.
- Breathe as you move.

Posture

Basic Arm Movements

Basic Arm Movements

Using an eight-count system:
We start the movement counting *one* and end the movement with *eight*.

Basic Up and Down

Arms come all the way up and go down

Starting with your arms at your sides, bring them up (palms facing down) for eight counts, ending with the arms above your head and the backs of the hands together.

Bring them down for eight counts until they are at your sides.

Arms come up with palms facing down

Arms in Second Position

Arms are extended from the shoulders

This is commonly used in dance and will be referred to throughout the book.

Second Position

Flip the Palms

Flip the palms halfway coming up and halfway going down

Starting with your arms at your sides, bring them up halfway for four counts, flip the palms to face up, and continue up for four more counts so that the arms are above your head and the palms are facing each other.

Reverse on the way down. Bring them down halfway for four counts, flip the palms to face down, and continue down for four more counts, so that your arms are at your sides.

Flip palms halfway up and halfway down

Arms Crossed in Front

Arms are crossed at chest

Arms Crossed Coming Down

Wrists crossed overhead

Starting with your arms at your sides, bring them all the way up (palms facing down) for eight counts.

Cross the wrists above your head, with the backs of the hands facing each other.

Continue to bring them down crossed in front of you, ending with your arms at your sides.

Arms crossed coming down

Arms Coming Up and Down the Centre

Arms down the centre of the body

As your arms come up above your head, flip the palms to face each other.

Bring the arms down through the centre of the body and along the sides of the hips.

End with your arms at your sides.

Palms facing each other

Arms Up (Wide V) Coming Down

Arms up in a wide V

At times the palms will be facing each other, and other times the backs of the hands will be facing each other.

To bring the arms down, flip the hands so that the backs of the hands are facing each other.

Bring arms straight down from the wide V until your arms are down at your sides.

Wide V

Arms Sweeping Across in Front Variations

Circle the arms toward you

Raise arms up from the sides to second position.

Sweep arms toward each other in front (palms down) to cross at the wrists.

Bring hands toward you.

Continue to move the arms down the centre of the body and along the sides of the hips.

Alternatively, bring your hands behind your neck to lift your hair.

Bring hands behind neck and sweep hair up

One-Arm Reach Forward Coming Up, Crossover, Flip toward You, and Down

Reach and crossover

With your right arm, reach forward and come up for eight counts.

Cross the back of the right hand to the left cheek for four counts.

Flip the right palm toward you and bring your right arm down through the centre for four more counts, ending with your right arm at your right side.

With your left arm, reach forward and come up for eight counts.

Cross the back of the left hand to the right cheek for four counts.

Flip the left palm toward you and bring your left arm down through the centre for four more counts, ending with your left arm at your left side.

Crossover

Shoulder Rolls

Rolling the shoulders backward in a circular motion

Start with the right shoulder sliding forward, up, back, and down. Repeat this a few times, and then connect all four points in a circular motion.

Repeat with the left shoulder, sliding forward, up, back, and down in a circular motion.

Continue alternating shoulders.

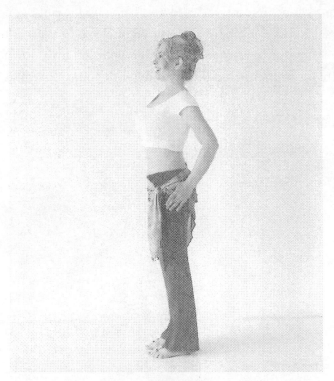

Rolling the shoulders backward

Basic Snake Arms

Arms engaged with shoulder rolls

Start with shoulder rolls.

Engage the arms by raising them at your sides and keeping the elbows below the shoulders.

As the shoulder goes back and down, the elbow and wrist bend gently in a soft, wavy motion.

Think in this order: shoulder, elbow, wrist, hand.

Rolling the shoulders backward with arms in second position

Egyptian Arms

Alternate extended arms, hand behind the ear

Extend one arm in front at chest level and the other with the hand behind the ear.

Alternate the arms.

Add a slight roll to the hands as they go back and forth.

Hand behind the ear

Egyptian Arms Variation

Alternate extended arms, hand at your temple

A variation is with one hand at your temple and the other extended forward.

Alternate the arms.

Add a slight roll to the hands as they go back and forth.

Hand at your temple

Egyptian Arms Sideways

Alternate extended arms in second

Another variation is with one hand at your temple and the other arm extending from the side in second position.

Alternate the arms.

Add a slight roll to the hands as they move side to side.

Arm in second position

Egyptian Arms Up

Arms up in a V position in front of you

With palms slightly facing you, bring one hand by your temple and extend the other arm in the V.
Alternate back and forth.

Hand by your temple, arm extended up

Arm Ripples
Wavy arms in front
Extend arms forward at chest level in front of you.
With relaxed elbows, bend at the wrists, with fingertips pointing up and down smoothly while alternating arms.
Add the shoulder rolls to bring the arm ripples up or down.

Gently bend wrists and elbows

Hand Ripples

Curl the fingers in and out

Place palms down and fingers together.

Lift only the fingers up and down, just as in the warm-up.

Continue this motion smoothly by curling your fingers in and out as if they were waves on the ocean.

Use your wrists to help the fingers come up and down.

Fingers curl smoothly

Wrist Rolls

Circles with the wrists

With arms at your sides, start rolling the wrists toward yourself.

Raise your arms up from the sides and above your head, ending with the backs of the hands facing each other.

Make sure to roll the wrists around and not just the hands. This is why your fingers face each other as you roll your wrists around.

With arms above your head and the backs of the hands facing each other (starting position), push the hands around in a circle while rolling the wrists. Keep the fingers tucked under as you roll the wrists continuously back to the starting position.

It is the rolling of the wrists all the way around from starting position to starting position that gives the hands their dynamic motion.

Try it with your arms extended straight in front of you, or at your sides extending straight out from your shoulders (second position).

Roll the wrists, starting position to starting position

Upper Body

Upper Body

Shoulder Slides

Shoulders moving front to back

Start with your hands on your hips.

Move the shoulders alternately from front to back, sliding straight through with no change in level.

Release the arms and continue.

Shoulder Shimmy

Shoulder slides alternating quickly

Start doing shoulder slides and then make them as fast as you can.

Slide the shoulders back and forth, sliding straight through with no change in level.

As you pick up speed, the movement becomes smaller.

Shoulder slides

Chest Lift

Lift and lower chest

Lift the upper chest up and bring it back down without raising the shoulders.

Lift upper chest

Chest Lock

Chest up and lock down

Move the chest up and down. Focus on the down, which is the lock.
Do not sink into the chest as it comes down; use your upper abdominal
muscles to keep you lifted. Check your posture.
Increase to double time: chest up and down, up, down.

Chest lock down

Chest Slides

Chest and ribcage move side to side
Slide the chest and ribcage side to side, without raising the shoulders, while keeping the lower body stationary.

Chest Circles

Drawing circles with the chest
Slide the chest and ribcage to the left side, up, to the right, and down at centre.
Repeat this smoothly and continuously.
Change direction. Slide the chest to the right side, up, left, and down at centre.

Chest side to side

Undulations

The undulation is S-shaped, like a snake

To start, lift the chest forward and up.

Pull the chest back by contracting your upper abdominal muscles and *then* your core muscles with relaxed knees.

Use your lower abdominal muscles to release the hips slightly back, elongating the torso, to bring yourself up.

Your chest should be up, preparing you to start over.

Forward and up

Contract abdominals to pull the chest back

Use lower abdominals to release the hips to start over

Lower Body

LOWER BODY

Basic Hip Accents

Lift hips alternating sides while centred

Shift your pelvis to neutral, so that it is underneath you and you are not leaning forward or backward. Your weight should be centred.

With relaxed knees, lift the hips alternating sides while keeping your weight centred. Your knees will move slightly.

Do not shift your weight from one side to the other.

Do not bend the knees back and forth, but keep them relaxed.

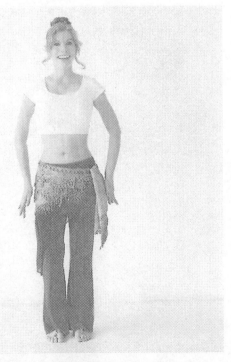

Weight centred, relaxed knees, lift hips alternating sides

Single Hip Accents

Hip moves up and down with bent knee

Face the right diagonal, with your weight on your right leg (supporting leg).

Bend your left knee, point the left toe on the floor, and raise your right arm.

Lift your left hip up and down, keeping the left knee bent.

Place your left foot on the floor to step and pivot to the other side.

Repeat in the left diagonal:

Face the left diagonal with your weight on your left leg (supporting leg).

Bend your right knee, point the right toe on the floor, and raise your left arm.

Lift your right hip up and down, keeping the right knee bent.

Place your right foot on the floor to step and pivot to the other side.

To end, place one foot beside the other foot, with your arms down.

Hip up and down with bent knee

Egyptian Shimmy

Thighs move back and forth quickly

To start, feet are hip width apart knees are relaxed, and your pelvis is in neutral (not tilting forward or backward).

Move your thighs back and forth, making sure your knees are relaxed underneath you and not locked behind you.

Pick up the pace; the movement of your thighs going back and forth becomes smaller as you go faster.

Thighs moving back and forth quickly

Hip Circle, Small

Circle with the pelvis

Place your feet hip width apart; have your knees relaxed and pelvis in neutral.

Circle your pelvis around using your lower abdominal muscles.

Reverse your direction.

Small circles with the pelvis

Twist Accents

Hips twist forward toward diagonals

Place feet hip width apart, relax the knees, and have pelvis in neutral.

Twist the left hip forward to the right diagonal, and then twist the right hip forward to the left diagonal.

Continue alternating hips, and pick up the pace.

You can also bend slightly down and up with the knees while twisting.

Another variation is to bend slightly through the centre while twisting from one diagonal to the other without arching your back.

Twist hips forward, diagonal to diagonal

Forward Figure 8

Hips moving in a figure-8 design

This is a beautiful movement in bellydance. Basically, you are drawing a horizontal number 8 on the floor using your hips. You will be using all four diagonals: the front right and left and the back right and left.

It consists of four parts: twist, slide, twist, slide. You have to use the four in that order to get the shape of the figure 8.

Have feet hip width apart, heels on the floor, knees relaxed, and pelvis in neutral. Use your abdominal muscles to help keep you centred.

- Twist your right hip forward toward the front right diagonal.
- Slide your left hip back straight through to the back left diagonal.
- Twist your left hip forward toward the front left diagonal.
- Slide your right hip back straight through to the back right diagonal.

Quick review: twist right front, slide left back, twist left front, slide right back.

To ensure that your slides are smooth, slide straight through the centre without popping your belly, and keep your heels on the floor.

Twist front, slide back, twist front, slide back.

Twist, slide, twist, slide.

Hips twist forward

Backward Figure 8

Forward figure 8 in reverse

You are drawing a horizontal number 8 on the floor using your hips.
Feet hip width apart, heels on the floor, relaxed knees, pelvis in neutral,
and using your abdominal muscles to keep you centred.

- Twist your left hip backward toward the back left diagonal.
- Slide your right hip forward straight through to the front right diagonal.
- Twist your right hip backward toward the back right diagonal.
- Slide your left hip forward straight through to the front left diagonal.

Quick review: twist left back, slide right front, twist right back, slide left front.

Remember to use your abdominal muscles to keep you centred and to ensure smooth slides.

Keep your heels on the floor.

Twist back, slide front, twist back, slide front.

Twist, slide, twist, slide.

Hips twist backward

Hip Kicks

Hip up and down and releasing the foot forward

This is similar to the starting position for the single hip accents but you lift the hip up and slightly back when it comes down. Release the foot forward as soon as the hip comes down.

Using two sets of up, down, and back, focus on the down and back, releasing the foot forward on the second down and back.

Facing the right diagonal, shift your weight to the right leg, bend the left knee, and point the left toe on the floor.

Raise your right arm and extend your left arm to the side, in second position.

Lift your left hip up in order to bring it down and back (left hip up, down, and back), releasing the left foot forward at the same time on the second down and back.

Left hip up, down, and back; left hip up, down, and back, and release left foot forward on the second down and back.

Repeat on the other side: right hip up, down, and back; right hip up, down, and back, and release the right foot forward on the second down and back.

Quick review: hip up, down, up, down, and release foot forward. Focus on the down movement of the hip. Down, down and release foot forward.

Hip down, down release

Hip Slides

Shift your weight side to side

Have feet hip width apart, knees relaxed, and pelvis in neutral.

Shift your weight side to side, using your abdominal muscles to help you stabilize as you move.

Your heels should be on the floor and your knees should be moving together (side to side) as you shift.

Make sure you are *not* bending your knees back and forth.

Shift straight through the centre without popping your belly.

Shift weight with knees moving together side to side

Directional Steps

DIRECTIONAL STEPS

Steps to change direction

Basic Turn

One rotation using four counts

Keep your feet underneath you, and pivot on the balls of your feet as you turn. This will help you turn faster and avoid a leg lock.

You also need to spot the diagonals so that you can turn without getting dizzy and establish starting and ending points.

Let's look at the footwork first. To turn right: step to the right with the right foot and pivot, step left foot and pivot, step right, and step left, to bring the feet together.

Quick review: take small steps as your feet pivot around to turn.
Step right, left, right, and left, to bring feet together.
Reverse: step left, right, left, and right, to bring feet together.

Pivot the feet as you turn

Spotting
Starting and ending point for turns

Spotting the diagonals (or corners) helps you turn without getting dizzy. It also gives your rotation a starting and an ending point. When you turn, your head will be the last to leave but the first to come around. For the left diagonal, look at a spot in the corner, step left, and start to turn around. Keep looking at that spot as your body turns. Your head comes around first, and you complete your turn looking at that same spot as you bring your body around.

Quick review: head is the last to leave but the first to come around when you turn.

Look at a spot in the corner and start turning for the first two counts. Bring the head around by the third count and the body around for the fourth count.

Half Turn

One rotation divided in half

Pivot on one foot halfway around to the back wall and then halfway around to the front wall, completing one full rotation in two parts.

Pivot on the front of the foot, not the heel.

For a half turn to the left, one pivot on the ball of your left foot to face the back wall, and then one pivot on the ball of your left foot to face front.

For a half turn to the right, one pivot on the ball of your right foot to face the back wall, and then one pivot on the ball of your right foot to face front.

Quick review: one pivot left to the back wall, one pivot left to the front wall.

Reverse your direction: one pivot right to the back wall, one pivot right to face front.

One pivot around to the back or front wall

Quarter Turn

One rotation divided into quarters

Pivot on one foot around the four walls of the room, completing one full rotation in four parts.

Pivot on the front of the foot, not the heel.

For quarter turns to the right: pivot on your right foot to face the right wall, pivot on your right foot to face the back wall, pivot on your right foot to face the left wall, pivot on your right foot to face front.

For quarter turns to the left: pivot on your left foot to face the left wall, pivot on your left foot to face the back wall, pivot on your left foot to face the right wall, pivot on your left foot to face front.

Quick review: pivot right to the right wall, pivot right to the back wall, pivot right to the left wall, pivot right to face the front wall.

Reverse: pivot left to the left wall, pivot left to the back wall, pivot left to the right wall, pivot left to face the front wall.

Pivot around the four walls, completing one rotation

Short Grapevine Step

Cross step to change diagonals

This versatile step is somewhat stationary but gives the illusion of a travelling step on the spot. There are four counts to this step.

Cross the right foot over the left foot. The left foot steps to the left; the right foot steps behind the left; and the left heel comes off the floor, with the toe on the floor facing the front right diagonal.

Reverse: cross left foot over right foot. The right foot steps to the right; the left foot steps behind the right; the right heel comes off the floor, with the toe on the floor to face the front left diagonal.

If you take small steps, it will be a directional step.

Large steps will give you the illusion of a travelling step.

Quick review: cross, step, back, touch.

Cross, step, back, touch toe

Travelling Steps

TRAVELLING STEPS

Grapevine

Cross step to travel

Travel to the left: cross the right foot over the left foot, left foot steps to the left, right foot steps behind left foot, left foot steps to the left.

Continue the pattern, or place your right heel on the floor to reverse your direction or to stop.

Travel to the right: cross the left foot over the right foot, right foot steps to the right, left foot steps behind the right foot, right foot steps to the right.

Continue the pattern, or place the left heel on the floor to reverse your direction or to stop.

Quick review: cross, step, back, step, cross, step, back, step, and place the heel down.

Reverse direction.

Cross, step, back, step

Tiptoe Walk

Walk on your toes

Walk on your toes and sway your hips side to side.

Step right and sway the right hip; step left and sway the left hip.

Keep your knees relaxed so that the hips can sway from side to side.

This looks great when you are walking around in a big circle.

Walking on your toes, swaying your hips

Step-Touch Walk

Step and point toe on the floor

This basic step has impact when used with your arms in second position or with your arms coming all the way up and then down.

To start, step on the right foot, touch left toe on the floor, now step with the left foot, and touch the right toe on the floor.

You can travel forward or backward and use any of the diagonals.

Quick review: Walk forward.

Take a step forward, touch front with opposite; other foot step forward, touch front with opposite.

Walk backward. Step back and touch front with opposite; step back, touch front with opposite.

Step, touch, step, touch.

Step, touch toe, step, touch toe

Egyptian Walk

The step-touch walk, adding the hips and the arms

Have the right arm and leg forward or left arm and leg forward.

Start the step-touch walk on the spot.

Add the hip accent, coming *up* on the touch.

Add the Egyptian arms (one arm extending forward).

Step right and touch left foot, with your left arm extended forward and right hand behind your ear.

Step left, touch right foot with your right arm extended forward and left hand behind your ear.

Walk forward for eight counts.

Step forward and touch front.

Walk backward for eight counts.

Step back and touch front.

Same arm and leg forward

Boray Shimmy

Shimmy on your toes

This shimmy allows you to travel while on your toes; you will generally move from one side to the other or in a circle.

Start with the Egyptian shimmy and come up onto your toes, with your arms in second position.

With relaxed knees, place one foot in front of the other.

You will notice that the shimmy changes, with the hips moving side to side.

Travel left with your right foot in front.

Travel right with your left foot in front.

Travel in a circle to the right with the right foot in front.

Travel in a circle to the left with the left foot in front.

Travel in a circle with feet together.

Shimmy on your toes

Introduction to Veil

INTRODUCTION TO VEIL

Fabric

Silk chiffon, silk crêpe de Chine, or pongee silk three yards long and forty-five inches wide (standard).

Holding the Veil

Drape the fabric over your shoulders with equal amounts of fabric on either side. Check the points of the fabric in front, and adjust the veil if necessary.

Wrap one inch of fabric over your first finger and secure it with your thumb and middle finger.

Check points of fabric in front

Extend your arms to the sides so that you have enough fabric to work with and so it is not too taut or too loose.

Veil extended evenly

Walking with the Veil

Add the tiptoe walk with the following:

Drag the veil on the floor behind you.

Walk with arms extended at the sides (second position).

Hold your arms up in a wide V, and flick the fingers back and forth.

Flick the fingers

Wing Flutter

Flick the veil

Bring your arms up and down, flicking the veil with your wrists as it rises up.

Flick wrists when arms are up

Twirling the Veil around You

Veil around to the front and around to the back

Bring the veil around to the front from the back and around to the back from the front continuously. Think in terms of one full rotation.

With veil behind, raise the right arm and bring the veil around to the left and in front as it circles down.

Now raise the left arm toward the right diagonal, and bring the veil around to the back.

Reverse your direction.

Raise the left arm up and bring veil around to the right and in front as it circles down. Now raise the right arm toward the left diagonal and bring the veil around to the back.

Twirling from back to front

Basic Turn with the Veil

Turn in four counts, with the veil behind

Turn to the right and step right, left, right. Extend left leg, and touch left toe on the floor for the count of four, with arms extended.

Reverse your direction: step left, right, left. Extend right leg, and touch right toe on the floor with arms extended.

Leg extended for count of four

Basic Turn into the Veil

Basic turn and raising one arm above your head

To turn to the right, step right and raise the right arm above your head, with the palm facing down and the left arm in second.

Turn into the veil and open your right arm down to second as you come around to the front.

Reverse: to turn to the left, step left, raise the left arm above your head with the palm facing down and the right arm in second.

Turn into the veil and open your left arm down to second as you come around to the front.

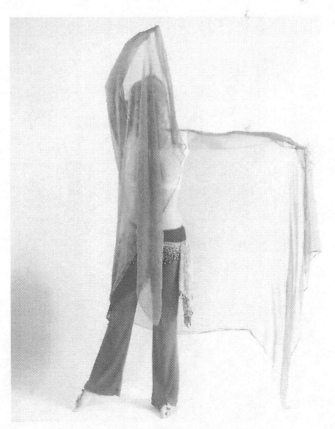

Arm up and arm in second position

The Draped Veil

Crossing arm and extending arm simultaneously

In slow motion, cross the right wrist over the left wrist.

Slide the right hand up to rest in *front* of the left shoulder, and extend the left arm out to the left side. The veil hanging should be draped.

Reverse: untwirl the veil in front. Cross the left wrist over the right wrist.

Slide the left hand up to rest in *front* of the right shoulder and extend the right arm out to the right side.

Quick review: cross wrists, slide hand to shoulder, and extend arm simultaneously.

Cross, slide, and extend.

Cross wrists

The veil, hanging loosely, should be draped.

The draped veil

The Flipped Veil

Veil is flipped and draped across the shoulders

With veil in front and dragging on the floor, toss it up onto your shoulders while still holding it.

You can lean back slightly, with one foot behind the other.

Lift your chin so that the veil drapes across your shoulders, and then bring your chin down immediately once the veil is in place.

Toss veil up onto shoulders

The veil should be draped across the shoulders.

Veil flipped and draped

Releasing the Flip, One Side

Reverse flip of one side of the veil

Step left to the left diagonal and extend the right leg, pointing your toes. Release the right side of the veil by flipping it downward while still holding the veil.

Place your right heel down, and pivot on the right foot to the right diagonal. Extend the left leg, pointing your toes. Release the left side of the veil by flipping it downward while still holding the veil

Place your left heel on the floor.

Reverse flip (down)

Releasing the Veil

Release the veil with a basic turn

With the veil behind you, step into a basic turn, and bring both arms behind you as you come around to face front.

Take the veil in one hand. Toss it off to the side or to the back of the room so that it will not interfere with your dancing.

Veil behind and basic turn

Veil in Front, Toss Behind

Toss behind with one hand

While walking backward, drag the veil on the floor in front of you.
Release one side of the veil, and hold it with the other hand.
Toss the veil behind you to release it, and step forward.

Toss behind

Veil in Front, Toss Up

Toss veil overhead

Drag the veil on the floor in front of you while walking backward.
Take the veil in one hand and toss it up and over your head to release it.
Walk forward and away from the veil.

Toss overhead

Cool-Down

You can add this sequence to your favourite cool-down.

- Place feet wide apart, with toes pointing outward. Bend at the knees without lifting your backside, squeezing the glutes as you come up. Repeat two more times.
- With knees bent, bring the right arm up from the right side and circle over to the left side. Hold ten seconds, and circle down and back to the right.
- With knees bent, bring the left arm up from the left side and circle over to the right side. Hold ten seconds, and circle down and back to the left.
- With knees bent, slowly roll down and place your hands on the floor.
- Bend and straighten the knees gently. Do this three times.
- With knees bent, slowly roll up to a standing position, ending with the arms reaching for the ceiling and feet together.
- Gently bend the right knee forward and reach up with the right arm.
- Gently bend the left knee forward and reach up with the left arm.
- Point and flex the toes (toward the knees and then down).
- Bend knee up and hold with both hands. Change knees and repeat.
- Bend knee back and hold foot behind you. Change knees and repeat.
- Gently tilt the head to the right side, to the left side, and to the front, looking down. Place one hand behind your neck and look up. Roll your head around one way, and then reverse.

Sessions

SESSIONS

Posture

Place feet hip width apart. Pelvis is in neutral, and knees and shoulders are relaxed. Fingers should be slightly fanned, with the thumb beside the index finger.

Using the Diagonal

These are the four corners of the room: the front left and right and the back left and right.

In bellydance, we often face the front diagonal because it showcases the movements nicely with an S-shaped three-quarter profile of the body.

Beats

Use an eight-count system to start and finish movements, or two sets of four counts. For example, four counts for one basic turn, and four counts for an Egyptian shimmy to complete the sequence. At times, you will use six counts plus two counts for a total of eight counts.

Transitions

When transitioning from one movement to another, remember to complete each movement before starting the next one.

Also, remember to place your heel down when you are travelling with the grapevine step and end in one diagonal while preparing to grapevine to the other diagonal.

Summary

I recommend doing each session twice a week. When you have completed all seven sessions, start again with session one and repeat all seven sessions. Continue to session eight.

When you feel ready to move forward, select a few combination sets, from the next section of the book, to create your own choreography.

Have fun!

Session 1

Warm-Up

Basic Arm Movements

Arms up for eight counts and down for eight counts
Flip of the palms
Arms in second (extended from the sides)
One arm reach forward and up, crossover, flip toward you, and down
Arms all the way up and crossed coming down
Egyptian arms: one arm extended forward and the other with the hand behind the ear or by your temple

Shoulder Rolls

Snake Arms

Basic Hip Accents

Step-Touch Walk with Arms in Second

Egyptian Walk

Egyptian Shimmy

Shimmy Set, One Minute

Combinations

Arms up with basic hip accents, for eight counts
Arms down, with basic hip accents, for eight counts
Step-touch walk for four counts and shoulder rolls for four counts
Egyptian walk for four counts and Egyptian shimmy for four counts

Veil

Holding the veil
Walking with the veil
Walking with arms up in a V and flicking the fingers
Wing Flutter
Twirling the veil around from front to back
The Draped veil

Cool-Down

NOTES

Session 2

Warm-Up

Review Session 1

Arm Ripples

Hand Ripples

Shoulder Slides

Shoulder Shimmy

Forward Figure 8

Backward Figure 8

Twist Accents

Shimmy Set, One Minute

Combinations

One forward figure 8 for four counts and twist accents for four counts
One backward figure 8 for four counts and Egyptian shimmy for four counts
One arm reach forward and up for eight counts; crossover for four counts; hand ripples across from shoulder to shoulder for two counts, and down for two counts

Cool-Down

NOTES

Session 3

Warm-Up

Review Session 2

Wrist Rolls

Chest Slides

Chest Lift

Chest Lock

Single Hip Accents

Basic Turn

Boray Shimmy

Shimmy Set, One and a Half Minutes

Combinations

Basic turn for four counts, and two chest locks for four counts
Single hip accents for four counts, and place heel down; Egyptian shimmy for four counts
Boray shimmy going left for four counts, reverse, and Boray shimmy going right for four counts

Veil

Basic turn
Basic turn into the veil

Cool-Down

NOTES

Session 4

Warm-Up

Review Session 3

Arms

Arms come up to a wide V and then down from a wide V

Chest Circle

Hip Circle, Small

Half Turn

Quarter Turn

Tiptoe Walk

Shimmy Set, One and a Half Minutes

Combinations

Half turn to the back for two counts, arms up for two counts, and half turn to the front for two counts (one complete rotation); bring arms down from the sides for two counts

Quarter turn and shoulder shimmy, four times (one complete rotation)

Tiptoe walk around in your own circle for six counts; heels on the floor and Egyptian shimmy for two counts

Chest circle for four counts, and one small hip circle for four counts

Cool-Down

NOTES

Session 5

Warm-Up

Review Session 4

Egyptian Arm Variations

Egyptian arms up
Egyptian arms to the side

Undulations

Hip Slides

Short Grapevine

Shimmy Set, Two Minutes

Combinations

Two hip slides with arms in second for four counts, and two hip slides with Egyptian arms to the side (same arm extended with same hip shifting) for four counts

One short grapevine step for four counts, and shoulder shimmy for four counts

Two undulations for four counts, and Egyptian shimmy for four counts

Veil

The flipped veil
Releasing the flip, one side
Releasing the veil

Cool-Down

NOTES

Session 6

Warm-Up

Review Session 5

Arm Sweeps

Arms Coming Down Centre

Hip Kicks

Grapevine

Shimmy Set, Two Minutes

Combinations

Shimmy with arms all the way up for eight counts, and arms down the centre (palms facing each other) and along the hips for eight counts

One grapevine step for four counts, and two undulations for four counts

Two hip kicks for four counts, and Egyptian shimmy for four counts

Cool-Down

NOTES

SESSION 7

Warm-Up

Review Sessions 1–6

Veil: Review Sessions 1, 3, 5

Shimmy Set, Two and a Half Minutes

Cool-Down

NOTES

Session 8

Warm-Up

Combinations
Add two sets of combinations (four movements)

Veil
Add two sets of veil combinations

Shimmy Set, Three Minutes

Cool-Down

NOTES

Combinations

COMBINATIONS

Basic hip accents, with arms coming up through second
Basic hip accents and forward figure 8
Hip circle, small and forward figure 8
Arms sweeping across in front with forward figure 8
Egyptian shimmy with arms coming down through the centre
Egyptian shimmy with arms coming down, crossing in front
Egyptian shimmy and twist accents
Twist accents stepping diagonal to diagonal
Egyptian Walk for four counts and basic turn
Egyptian Walk for four counts and Egyptian Shimmy
Shoulder shimmy and Egyptian shimmy
Shoulder shimmy and basic snake arms
Basic snake arms and shoulder rolls
Tiptoe walk in a circle and basic turn
Chest slides and one chest circle
Chest circle and undulation
Undulation and chest lock
Grapevine step and basic snake arms
Grapevine step and shoulder shimmy
Hip kicks and Egyptian shimmy
Short grapevine step and hip kicks
Short grapevine step and arm ripples
Short grapevine step and single hip accents
Arms up in wide V and coming down with backward figure 8
Hip slides and backward figure 8
Hip slides and Egyptian arms sideways (extended in second)
Half turn to back and to front
Half turn to back and Boray shimmy (on toes)
Boray shimmy travelling in a circle
Step-touch walk backward with Egyptian arms up

Quarter turn and Egyptian shimmy for one full rotation
Wrist rolls coming down and arm ripples
One arm up, crossover, flip toward you and down, and undulation
One arm up, crossover, hand ripple across and down

Combinations with Veil

Tiptoe walk dragging the veil
Tiptoe walk with arms in second, and basic turn
Tiptoe walk, arms up in a wide V, and flick the fingers
Tip toe walk with arms up in a wide V and wing flutter
Tiptoe walk, arms up, and basic turn
Basic turn right and basic turn left
Basic turn and basic turn into the veil in opposite direction
Twirling the veil from the back to the front, and flip the veil
Twirling the veil from front to back and basic turn
Flipping the veil over shoulders, grapevine, release one side, and reverse
Flipping the veil over shoulders, basic turn, release one side, and reverse
Veil behind, coming up with arms in wide V, and forward figure 8
Veil in front, coming up with arms in second, and backward figure 8
The draped veil and follow your arm around in a circle, reverse
Basic turn, twirling the veil around to the front, and chest circle
Basic turn, twirling the veil around to the back, and small hip circle
Turning into the veil, and undulations
Releasing the veil with a basic turn, and Egyptian shimmy
Releasing the veil, tossing it behind, and Egyptian walks
Releasing the veil, tossing it up overhead, and hip kicks

Glossary

Basic Arm Movements

Basic up and down
Arms in second
Flip the palms
Arms crossed in front
Arms crossed coming down
Arms coming up and down centre
Arms up (wide V) coming down
Arms sweeping across in front variations
One arm reach forward, crossover, flip toward you, and down
Shoulder rolls
Basic snake arms
Egyptian arms with hand behind the ear
Egyptian arms with hand at your temple
Egyptian arms sideways
Egyptian arms up
Arm ripples
Hand ripples
Wrist rolls

Upper Body

Shoulder slides
Shoulder shimmy
Chest lift
Chest lock
Chest slides
Chest circles
Undulations

Lower Body

Basic hip accents
Single hip accents
Egyptian shimmy
Hip circle, small
Twist accents
Forward figure 8
Backward figure 8
Hip kicks
Hip slides

Directional Steps

Basic turn
Spotting
Half turn
Quarter turn
Short grapevine step

Travelling Steps

Grapevine
Tiptoe walk
Step-touch walk
Egyptian walk
Boray shimmy

Introduction to Veil

Fabric
Holding the veil
Walking with the veil
Wing Flutter
Twirling the veil around you
Basic turn with the veil

Basic turn into the veil
The draped veil
The flipped veil
Releasing the flip, one side
Releasing the veil with a basic turn
Releasing the veil, toss behind
Releasing the veil, toss up

Resources

Organizations
www.mecda.org
www.medabellydance.com

Bulletin Boards
www.groups.yahoo.com/group/raks_toronto
www.bhuz.com

Music
www.hollywoodmusiccenter.com
www.hossamramzy.com
www.natacha-atlas.com
www.cdbaby.com/artist/georgedimitrisawa
www.suleimanwarwar.com

Dancewear
www.bellydance.com
www.malabar.net
www.capezio.com
www.danskin.com
www.lululemon.com

Costumes
www.turquoiseintl.com
www.sharifwear.com

Magazines

www.gildedserpent.com
www.zaghareet.freeservers.com
www.shimmyspiritofdance.com
www.yallahmagazine.com

About the Author

www.evyeniakarmi.com

Evyenia Karmi lives in Toronto, Ontario, Canada, and teaches bellydance for the city of Toronto. She has been dancing for twenty years and has performed regularly for the Greek, Turkish, East Indian, and Arabic communities. As a member of the International Dance Council, Evyenia continues to perform in theatres and festivals. This is her first book.

Acknowledgments

I thank my wonderful family for always being at my side.

I am grateful to my teacher, Tahia Sassine, for sharing her incredible talent and knowledge.

I am inspired by my students, with their enthusiasm, excellent attendance, and constant asking for my instructional notes.

I appreciate my peers and all of you who keep this dance form alive.

I thank Johnny Bergeron for supporting artists during their creation process.

I appreciate the city of Toronto for its cultural diversity.

I thank Peter Bourikos for his input on Greek social studies.

Thank you to my PR assistant, P. Charles.

I say *merci* to my friends and relatives for giving me their precious time.

I thank my publishing team: Amy McHargue, Meredith Lefkoff, Rebekka P., Sarah Disbrow and Alexandra Jones for their leadership, guidance, and patience.

I am indebted to my mentor, Tasso Lakas. Thank you for encouraging me to write.

Afterword

My journey in the bellydance world has been so rewarding. It all started with a writing project in 1992, when I was searching for information on this dance form. Twenty years later, I am happy to share what I have learned, through this instructional book. These basic steps are used by enthusiasts and professionals alike. This is the starting point that will provide you with the fundamental dance steps and help prepare you to advance to the next stage. I have created choreography using these core steps. I hope you are inspired to take a class or to continue studying this beautiful and ageless dance form.

Evyenia Karmi